How to Write and Publish a Book in Your Spare Time

By

Nancy Fornataro

How to Write and Publish a Book in Your Spare Time

Copyright © 2017 by Nancy Fornataro

Table of Contents

Chapter 1

The Making of a Writer

You've probably bought this book for some very good reasons. You are becoming obsessed with writing a book. Or you know you could write a good romance or detective story. Maybe you want to make some extra money, or you're trying to mentally escape from a less than wonderful life, or both.

All valid reasons, and I hope I can help each and every one of you to realize your dreams. That is my primary goal here. I want to help you make a footprint in the world. Because of physical limitations, I'm not able to write and publish like I once did. But this book is important to me because I will share with you lessons I've learned, and I'm hoping to assist you along your path to becoming a best-selling writer!

So what constitutes an author? If I had to pick one character trait of a good and prolific writer, I would say determination. All those hours spent in front of a computer screen, or sometimes scribbling on a pad and paper, take dogged determination.

When I started writing, it was 1983. After reading thousands of romance novels, I thought I could do a great thing if I just wrote a novel that, as a reader, I would enjoy. It was a romance set in Jamaica and England. After researching extensively, as I'd never been to Jamaica and needed historical details, I developed a loose plot.

Anyway, I painstakingly wrote the book in longhand on yellow pads and then typed it on (the dreaded) onion skin paper. What a chore. There was no word processing to check my spelling back then. I kept a dictionary handy, and I used White Out for errors.

After sending the manuscript snail mail to several publishers, where it was rejected, I gave up the idea of publishing but still kept a hard copy of the book for years. When I bought a word processor in 1994, retyped the book into it, and saved the file on small square floppies, I threw away the hard copy. And a few years later, the unthinkable happened. I'd stored the floppies in a less than climate controlled spot, and *they were all no good.* So that book is lost forever. I'm surprised I ever wrote anything again after that.

But I did write again. Why? I'm obsessed with storytelling. And I don't care what happens, I will keep writing. It's hard, demanding, sometimes tricky work but oh, so worth it when I'm able to crank that 'baby' out!! And in the end, it is actually like giving birth, as it takes months, and sometimes years, of work to publish.

I use this saying quite often: *For everything you want in life, you have to give up something else.* Let's think about that for a minute. If you want to be slim, you need to give up fattening foods and stop overeating. If you want to be financially secure, you need to stop spending so much money. If you want to get a higher paying job, you need to spruce up your resume and give up that 'secure' job you're hanging onto.

So, if you want to become a writer, *you need to give up tons of time*. Writing is the original Time Bandit. Once you go into right brain (more about that later) you totally lose track of time. Hours and days go by in a flash and a blur. Weekends, weeknights, and time with your family and friends goes as well.

You give up your physical well-being, as your neck and back might hurt from hunkering in front of the computer. You may give up your vacation time from your job just to publish or work on the book. Self-publishing might require an infusion of cash to promote your book with ads or buying the rights to a photo to use on your cover. Also, in the case of bad reviews, it could cause you to give up your self-confidence (hopefully that would be just a temporary setback!!).

So, ask yourself these questions: Am I willing to give up my time, money, family, friends, well-being, vacations and self-confidence? If so, I hereby dub you an official Writer. So get your excuses ready, and prepare for a bumpy ride.

Chapter 2

Supreme Supplies, Perfect Preparation

There are certain preparations you'll need to make before you begin to write. (This is the perfect excuse to procrastinate, which is one of the biggest downfalls of umpteen writers, so don't spend too much time here...)

Supplies you will probably need:

A working laptop computer with Word or some type of word processing program with spell-check. It will make your writing so much easier to have that ever-present spelling check, although it can be annoying with slang dialogue!! If your finances are tight, try the second-hand computer stores, or even Goodwill for inexpensive computers.

Make sure you have *access to the internet*, as this comes in so handy for research, and contacting agents as well as book publishers.

A desk with ample storage space. I know the corner, glass desks are cool looking, but they have zero storage. I found that out the hard way. Now I have a roll-top desk with eight drawers.

Blue or black pens (I once overdid this to the extreme and ended up with about two hundred pens. True story. I hit the back to school specials really hard that year! So in three years, the household 'black hole' has swallowed up most of them...)

Red pens for editing.

Pencils, regular or mechanical.

Several regular *8-1/2 X 11 lined pads*. There may be a time when your computer is not accessible and you are chocked full of wonderful, creative ideas. Or you may just prefer to write in longhand, then transcribe into the computer. Over the years, I've learned to type into the computer when I go into my right brain hazes, but that is a bit tough for a new writer.

Small 2" X 4" notebooks. Keep these by your bedside and with you during the day in a purse or pocket for ideas you get while not at your computer.

Several packs of 3" X 5" white and colored index cards. I use these all the time for non-fiction books, and they are very motivating if I'm not sure what approach to take on a subject.

A stapler.

Large, stretchy rubber bands. Handy for binding the manuscripts requested by publishers.

Paper clips, large and small.

And if you're the organized type, buy *a 2" three-ring notebook* with dividers. (Be careful here, you can spend all your time getting organized and no time actually writing.) You could make sections for Characters, Chapters, Plot Ideas, Timeline, Historical Notes, etc.

One more item I find useful for notes along the way for character development and all-important character names are either steno pads or *thin 8-1/2" X 11" spiral bound notebooks*, one for each novel, so your messy notes stay in one place.

So, in a basic way, stock up on office supplies.

The second part of preparing to write is finding a place or quiet *corner conducive to writing*. This place is where you can let your hair down, relax, rejuvenate and be creative.

Some suggestions:

A guest room or den in your house where a door can shut out noise and nosy kids/spouses. This is ideal because you can also have your desk in there, along with writing supplies. Over the years, because I don't have this luxury anymore (my desk is now in a kitchen corner), I've learned to blank out the interfering spouse and perfected the art of dirty looks.

If you live in a warm climate, *an outside porch* with a comfortable chair is nice, barring neighbor's lawn mowers and salutations.

If all your bedrooms are crammed with a bumper crop of kids, you might want to eke out a bit of room in *your own bedroom*, a corner where you can either plant your desk or a comfy chair. Again, you can shut the door and put a Do Not Disturb sign out there. (Be sure to share with your spouse your aspirations to be a writer and make sure she/he understands. And kids should be taught not to interrupt you; knowing their boundaries is good for them!)

If you're in a roommate situation and they are noisy and uncooperative, *the public library* is a great place to find quiet time. Or, if you're unable to write at home, either temporarily or all the time, try writing at your *workplace*. During lunch hours, or before or after work, all you need is a quiet corner.

Where there's a will, there's a way. Get creative.

A few years after I married my hubby, I was working full-time and busy being a stepmom. I'd get up at four in the morning, write my novel pages longhand on a pad for a few hours, then transcribe my writing when I got home, which took another hour or so. So I managed to squeeze writing in there. I mean, what other dope would get up at four in the morning!! It was super quiet and it was a good writing habit I practiced.

And the last supply item I'd suggest would be *earphones* either to wear to block out noise or to listen to music while you're writing. Actually I have certain CD's I will forever associate with certain books I wrote. I listened to them over and over again, and it even helps me to get back into my writing and finish the books.

Chapter 3

How to Start

Okay, I've put off this chapter long enough!! True confessions. I hate starting. I can pick up where I left off with no problem, but actually beginning is the hard part.

Procrastination is the worst habit a writer can have. Although, I do know writers who write ten pages a day consistently, even if they throw out the pages the next day. That's the perfect approach. Keep in practice. Make progress.

Some days, I can think of so much stuff to do other than writing my pages: cleaning the fridge, mopping the kitchen, reading the newspaper, shopping the internet, reading Facebook pages, 'liking' on Instagram. You name it, anything works as a good excuse.

(Although, at times, I do have the cleanest house on the block.)

BUT, eventually I remind myself that if I'm consistent in my writing, I can publish more books. *The journey of a thousand miles begins with a single step.* Page after page gets created, and obviously the first draft is not perfect, but that's why we edit, yes? And as long as I'm on this subject, let me make this plea: Do NOT be so in love with your writing that you cannot delete or revise portions of your manuscripts. More about this later.

So how to begin? Write one page, typed, which is about 250 words. That's not much. Just get it done. Nail down that wonderful beginning you've been thinking about. And don't be picky and perfectionistic, just write it. You can edit the next day.

Say you're writing a fiction romance. Woman meets man and sparks fly. But, you ask, how do I start it? Ask yourself these questions: Who, What, Where, When and How? This alone should get you going.

Continue your questions: Where are they? Who are they? Occupations? Quirks? Get a general idea, and yes, you can make character names and descriptions on paper but I'd advise you to make them loose. Otherwise, your characters can't grow and evolve when you're in right brain. I've had characters say and do things in my stories that I *never* expected.

Which brings me to a fun oddity: *Right Brain*!! You may think you have never been in right brain, but I doubt it. Think of it this way: when you ride along in your car, bored, thinking about anything but driving (like how you'd try out for The Voice or something) and suddenly you 'come to' and realize you've almost hit the car in front of you, you have been in right brain. (And that gets dangerous unless you're in your writer's chair, by the way.)

The more bored you are, the more you will be in right brain. The brain is a very active part of our bodies, and it hates to be inactive. If you have writer's block, take a walk around the neighborhood. Go for a ride in the country. Take a short trip. By the time you get back, you'll be full of wonderful ideas.

Another good method for writer's block, and writer's inability to finish, is to edit your work. As you read it over, more and more ideas will come to you. If the book is very long, just read the last few pages you've written, which gets you back in the writing mode.

Writing in right brain is like you're seeing a movie in slow motion, and then writing or typing as fast as you can to describe it. I'm a visual person, so if I try to orally transcribe what I'm seeing, that just doesn't work for me. Although if you're a very talkative person, that might be your method. Whatever works best for you is the optimal solution.

To me, the most fascinating part of writing is how our brains continue to 'work' on plotting and character development while we are not in our writer's space.

I vividly remember when I thought I'd finished Lacene Lords, my paranormal book, and hubby and I went to Hawaii for a week. Well, I brought some writing pads and pens, and discovered I needed them badly when all these thoughts about polishing the manuscript and plot came to me during that time. Parts I needed to change, even dialogue came to me in spurts and I was writing frantically, much to my husband's irritation.

So even though I thought I'd finished the dang book, it popped up in my problem-fixing right brain!!

Another imperative step in the beginning is to ask yourself what niche or category your book fits into. Niches in fiction include romance, drama, sci-fi, crime, detective, horror, women's fiction, contemporary literature, thrillers, etc. Please do not skip this step because although occasionally one oddball newbie book will hit the bestseller lists, this is rare. Most of the time readers search for books by category.

If you're writing a romance, what sub-type is it? Historical? Contemporary? Saga? Gay and Lesbian? Teen? When you go to publish this novel, you will be required to categorize it in detail, not just "Romance" or "Fiction" but a secondary category as well.

Also, an intriguing book title is all important to your success. I noticed something interesting in the newspaper today related to this. Most fiction bestsellers have titles with one to three words. Non-fiction bestsellers, for the most part, are the same. But what really interested me was the new book titles. New fiction titles had one to three words, no surprises there. But *new non-fiction titles had an average word count of fifteen*!! Not sure what this means, whether it's a trend or perhaps those titles are destined to be losers...

At times, I never know the title of my current book until I go to publish it. I believe I went through two hundred (really, seriously, on paper) ideas on titles for *Lacene Lords*. And don't ask where I found the word Lacene, because I don't know or remember. It actually means 'pigeon' but I liked the way it fit in there and that turned out to be the name of my fictional Arizona city. It worked out well.

Sometimes you have a series, like my *Dream Club* books, so I have The Dream Club #1 - Corpse, The Dream Club #2 - Hunted, and so on.

I like a catchy title, but sometimes simplicity is best: *Pyro* left no doubt about the fictional subject. But I did preface that title with *Whirlwind Passing*, as the book was part of a series.

How to Look Like a Million on Next to Nothing is one of my 'bread and butter' books, and has done pretty well. I couldn't believe no one had used that title!! I always search my book titles to make sure I don't duplicate what someone else has done. So Google your title, and search on Amazon. I think Amazon has just about every book offered for sale.

I've noticed the 'How to' titles are popular, along with 'Organize' and 'Minimalist' books.

Looking at this, I realize that with non-fiction books you're promising something. But with fictional books, the title needs to be really catchy. When readers are perusing the internet bookshelves, you have about two seconds to grab their attention with a curious title, an awesome cover, and another ten seconds to rope them in with your blurb or story recap.

Back on the subject of how to start, I prefer dialogue early on. Do not bore your readers with paragraph after paragraph of weather descriptions or worse yet, character descriptions. Weather and character descriptions can be *woven into* the story quite successfully.

Dialogue involves the reader, and if done correctly, can speak volumes about the character. Shoot your reader right into the action:

"I hate this," Dora sighed, as she waited impatiently. So now the reader is wondering just what she hates.

Her long legs shifted and her mouth drew into a pout, as her pink skirt rustled. So now our reader wonders, is she spoiled? Good-looking? And what's with the skirt? Where the heck is she?

You can draw the reader into the story with the five senses: sight, sound, smell, taste, and touch. If Dora is waiting backstage, maybe she's a dancer, and she could wrinkle her nose at the musty smell. (She's sounding more spoiled as I go along, maybe the hero will cure her of that, lol) Or there could be the sounds of stagehands yelling or props falling.

I think the easiest way to incorporate the senses in your writing is to just *close your eyes and pretend you are there.* I remember when I was working on the fiery end of

Lacene Lords just how hard it was to incorporate all the senses. I was so caught up in *visually* describing the fire that I forgot the smoke smell and the humongous sound of floors caving in, and even that my characters would probably feel the heat of it. It's a dimensional thing.

I don't know if there are any golfers out there, but Chevy Chase put it perfectly when he said, "Be the ball..." in the movie Caddyshack. So what I'm telling you is "Be the story!"

Chapter 4

Non-Fiction

Although fiction seems to be more popular in the writing communities, and we'll get to that in the next chapter, non-fiction needs to be mentioned.

There is a totally different approach to this genre. It is primarily left brain, in that it deals with facts. However, there is a bit of right brain going on there as well for title and book presentation.

Approach is everything in writing non-fiction books. Your title is super important, and should grab the reader right away. And the slant should be slightly different in your book than every other book in the genre. Something new. Something unique.

I'm reminded of a book I read this year (being a self-help book junkie) called The Curated Closet. What a title, it grabbed my attention right away. Curating a closet? That got me. And what a wonderful book, as well, it did not disappoint. I learned a tremendous amount about wardrobes in that book, more than every other 'closet' or 'wardrobe' book I've ever read. And I changed my perspective because of it.

This is what we're after with non-fiction writing. We want the reader to learn a few things from our books and appreciate us for it!!

My approach to non-fiction books is a series of index cards, with chapter numbers, and ideas I want to present. I usually write one idea on each card, then move them around until I'm satisfied that each idea is with the proper chapter. Then when I type, I use the cards as a general reference to expand on.

Some niches in the non-fiction realm are: self-help of all types, true crime, psychology, decorating, history, biography, science, math and so on.

If you know a lot about a subject, you should write about it. Perhaps if you have strong opinions on something, you can write about *that*. You just never know what will appeal to the public. Even the story of your life or a book of poems could interest some people.

Publishing a book looks great on a resume, for your given career track, as well as being lucrative. And yes, I really mean that!! My non-fiction books sell consistently, where usually the fiction books are a quick flash in the pan. So if you're after steady income, I'd suggest non-fiction of any type, as it never goes out of style. Just be sure you are really interested in the subject and your enthusiasm and knowledge will inspire the readers.

This is one instance where I'd tell you to outline. Type your chapter names and contents headers first, and you can refer back to them as you're writing. And buy 3 X 5 cards by the bucket load, because you'll need them. These little cards are so handy for self-motivation. If I'm feeling lazy or uninspired, I just grab my book index cards, which can usually fit in any type of index plastic file box, and sit on the couch and add information or re-shuffle them. It gets me involved with the book again.

And one last item for all types of writing is the research phase. Be sure to research everything about your book. If you're writing non-fiction, use your index cards and be sure to note the source of your information. Certain books will require a Bibliography.

Chapter 5

Fiction

Ah yes, fiction...this wonderful way to forget all your cares and escape your miserable life for a few hours. But wait, you don't *read* fiction? Yikes. You'll never know how to *write* fiction unless you *read* fiction. This is your starting point for good writing. Read fifty pages of someone else's work every day, in your given area, preferably best-sellers. By doing this, you'll understand what comprises good dialogue and plot. You'll understand pacing and cadence.

If you want to write fiction, the market is not only saturated, it is *over saturated*. There is an incredible amount of competition there, so be warned. Plus, people want to read best-sellers so they won't waste their money on what could be a crappy book. Makes sense to me. But this leaves us newbie authors in the wind.

However, there are always exceptions to the above, and that makes me happy. I love to see Indy authors (Indy=independent, publish-your-own-books authors) really make it big, and there have been plenty of great successes out there. It's what we all live for and hope for, not only for ourselves but our fellow authors as well.

Just for reference, I'd like to let you know that even if you should snag a publishing contract with a bona fide publisher, you will not go around the country for book signings, unless you arrange them yourself. And royalties are paid way after the fact, months or years. Also, if you get any advance, it will probably be small.

At any rate, fiction should be fun, fast and fabulous. Involve your reader. Have some wild characters! In Whirlwind Passing I loved

Mulligan, a psychic FBI detective, who came into subsequent Whirlwind books. I patterned his looks after John Goodman, and he had this snarky, mean personality which added to the stress of the hunt for a serial killer. But readers quickly understood he's gentle in spirit, and totally involved in his cases.

In a sense, you should pattern your characters after real people, as we do not live in a one dimensional world. People are complex. Not everyone is smart. Some are ugly. Some are truly vicious and mean. And everyone has their weaknesses and hang ups. However, your characters should also have a larger than life quality to them, maybe a bit exaggerated for effect.

Also, in a romance, or any other type of books for that matter, I love to see flaws in the characters. Right now I'm reading a Historical Romance, and the hero was badly shot, which caused him to have panic attacks a year later. This makes the story more realistic and believable.

In my *Romance for Angel - The Biker*, the lead heroine has these panic attacks. I researched it so I'd know just how she felt and acted when these attacks took place. I also had to research bikers, how they acted and their creeds and foibles.

In my book Pyro, I read extensively about pyromaniacs and how they operated, and firefighters, and what they went through at fires. Very, very interesting!! You might not use all the info you gather, but at least you'll be well informed so you can step into the shoes of the characters.

Actually, the research alone will give you plot ideas. Immerse yourself in the culture you're writing about. Plus it will let you see if you *want* to write about that culture. I wasn't really sure I wanted to write about bikers after reading about ten books on the subject. But I saw some ideals present there, like brotherhood, and I could relate. I'd worked in Laughlin in 2002 during the rumble between Hells Angels and Monguls. I had that story to tell. So some of the bikers in my book were heroes, and some were villains. All but one were loyal brothers. Just like real life. I worked it out.

In the end, fiction should take the reader to a place where he or she can't put the book down. Reader relates to the characters, feels empathy and loves the excitement of the story.

Chapter 6

To Plot or Not to Plot...

I attended a writer's conference one time, and all of us were supposed to share a few pages of our writing. This gets sticky because I found myself wanting to share, but not wanting to hear the criticism. I took a deep breath, shared, and when I was done, these wonderful people helped me with the prologue of *Lacene Lords*.

However, later in the day, a fellow shared his crime novel pages with us. His beginning contained weather descriptions, scenery descriptions, and worst of all, every known fact about all of his characters. OMG, no one knew what to say after he finished. Then another writer bit the bullet and said, "Man, that was boring. You need some dialogue in there." Or something to that effect. I could hear a sigh of relief go through the room.

And I'm sure the writer had outlined and gone through his plot the same way, probably mapped it out and all. But there was no spark there, and nothing vaguely interesting.

I always like to have a vision in mind for my books, but nothing specific. I do not plot. Like in *Romance in Vegas*, I knew I wanted a love story between a novice showgirl and the casino owner Scaletti, who I'd introduced as a character in *Pyro*. I just loved Scaletti and I wanted a book to focus on him and his hunk-i-ness!! But, that's all I knew when I first started writing this book. The story panned out in my mind from start to finish, like a movie.

If you let your brain do the plotting, it should come naturally to you, especially if you read lots of books. Even watching a TV show or movie can give you this: A beginning, a middle (where everything is tense) and an end, where loose ends are tied up tightly. Watch an episode of Bluebloods or other cop shows. Notice where the writers put you in the beginning, right in the action, and make note of the problems the characters experience. See how the TV writers wrap up the end, after the climax scene.

Of course, different books might require other approaches. When I wrote the climax scene in *Romance for Angel - The Biker*, I needed to watch the bootleg tape of the Hell's Angels and Monguls. About a hundred times. Then I had to write down a sequence of events and who was where during the action. I wanted it to be as real and factual as possible. So I guess you could say I let real life drive my climax scene, plus many parts of this book.

I say, for the most part, try to let your imagination have free reign. You might like the results. And, you might find things end up far differently than you'd planned for the details of the novel, as the characters say and do things you hadn't expected.

When I wrote *Lacene Lords* (which was part of the great 'floppy' disaster, where I lost chapter 8 and had to re-create it, GAH) I didn't even know who'd killed Spence's parents. I didn't decide who they'd be until I was two-thirds through writing the book. That way, if I didn't know who did the bad deed, my readers sure wouldn't!! And I didn't decide the ghosts were the ghosts until I was halfway through.

Your imagination is *very powerful*, so in the case of your writing, give it freedom. You will be astonished at how it works for you.

One tip I have for you, if you get stuck at a particular place in your book, is to ask the 'what if' question. Say your hero and heroine meet but there is no spark, and you can't seem to get it going. What if she douses him with a hose by mistake? Or runs her car into his? What if he doesn't want a romance, and is cold to her? What if they have to work together and neither one wants to? What if they feel an attraction, but he's her boss? Or she's his supervisor? Hiring him?

At any rate, you get the general idea. I wanted a different type of romance, so I asked myself if I could write a story with a blind hero. Thus *Romance for Matthew* was born! Challenge yourself. Paint yourself and your characters into a corner, then brainstorm out!!

Chapter 7

Characters I Have Known

I think it's true that you have to really get to know your characters. You need to sit in their shoes, feel what they're feeling, think what they're thinking, etc. Solid characterization is the key to good fiction. There is nothing worse in a fiction story than a one-dimensional character. Now it's true that for a side, rather non-important bit character you can fudge a little. We don't need to know his or her whole background. But the main characters must have substance. What drives them to do what they do? What happened in their pasts that caused them to act the way they do?

In my book *Pyro* the fire-setting character had been abandoned by his mother at an early age, and also branded by fire by her at an even earlier age. So to say he had psychological issues would be an understatement.

See the character in your mind. Is he nervous or calm? What quirks does he have? And please, *weave the character descriptions into the story*. Below I've written two very different descriptions of an old man.

Not so great:
Eli Smith was an 87 year old man. He lived in Las Vegas and had two children, Eli Junior and Evelyn. He also had four grandchildren, two by each child, a boy and a girl from each. His wife had died two months earlier, and he still grieved.

(For God's sake, please don't start out any story like that!!)

Better:
In the bedroom, Eli cussed as he tripped over his late wife's shoe. "How in tarnation

did that get there? Thought I got rid of all those things," he said.

Hearing the phone, he limped over and answered it. "What?"

"Dad? Why do you sound so out of breath?"

Eli decided not to mention the shoe, as his daughter Evelyn was still missing her mother. "Nothin.' How's the kids?"

This is rough, but hopefully you get the idea. Don't tell a boring story, bring the reader in. Involve your reader and provide some action.

I've got an assignment for you. Write the beginning of a short story (less daunting than a novel) and use one or more characters from your workplace or your private life, some people you know who are unusual and have a few quirks. Give them some dialogue. Don't name names, however, assign fake ones. Besides, this is just for your own use anyway. Exaggerate their mannerisms and oddities and see how it reads.

My Dad's quirks have appeared in a few characters in my books!! And lots of times I've merged two people into one character, maybe the physical makeup of one person and the personality of another. If you let your right brain handle this, you'll have no problems.

But all this aside, as I was reading a crime novel last night, I realized that in fiction, *the main character has to be likeable*. Yes, he or she has drama and problems and shortcomings, but the character must have substance with some of these qualities: honesty, fidelity, compassion for others, hard-working, caring, etc.

Now this being said, I can say I've read fiction where a heroine was a thief, a cop was a hard-ass, and so on. BUT there are always very good reasons why the character does what he does, and this is your job as the writer to weave this into the storyline.

One of my pet peeves with some fiction is the habits or expressions of the main characters repeated ad nausea. This can be disastrous to your story if you overdo it.

For instance, maybe one of your characters has a habit of saying "Dang." Or tapping his fingers on a table. Once in a while, let him say or do it, but don't have it appearing on every page!! A little goes a long way with that.

Chapter 8

Dialogue and POV

Another critical element of fiction is *believable* dialogue between the characters. If you're writing a crime novel, I'd encourage you to visit and 'shadow' detectives for a day at your local police station. Listen to how they speak, and expressions they use. If writing a book for teenagers, know their language and code words. Study up on this. You can even use the internet in some cases.

Don't be afraid for characters to interrupt each other. We all do it in real life. And, our voices trail off too...

I always love a book that begins with dialogue. In *Romance for Kinkade* I started it with, "Hellfire and damnation!" Then in *Romance for Angel - The Biker*, I began with "He told you I'm a backdoor man?"

A lot of books I read contain eighty percent dialogue, which seems a bit much, and the rest contains a little description. I'd say if you have around half your manuscript as dialogue, that's a good percentage. I like a certain amount of description in books, especially descriptions of the characters. Do they have brown hair, blue eyes, or what? Again, weave it into the story.

If you're writing a historical novel, before you even begin to write, read, read, read historical novels set in the time period you're interested in. See how the characters talk, what expressions they use. I'm not telling you to copy anything, but do immerse yourself in the time period. Then, when you begin writing, it will flow off your pen easily.

Novels set in modern day are so much easier. Listen to conversations around you every day. If you're writing about a romance, where the heroine works at a bakery, hang out at bakeries and get with the lingo.

There is a common thread here, and that is research, research, and research more. It's the only way your story will be the slightest bit believable.

And if you're not sure whether your dialogue sounds credible, get a friend and read each other the lines of dialogue to see if they sound right. You'd be surprised at how hokey some phrases sound when you read them out loud!

Back to the bakery, ask the women who work there what their work problems are, as well. Chat them up. Tell them you're writing a novel, and they'll be thrilled for their knowledge to be included! Plus it's a great way to make contacts and sell your book when it's finished.

Writing is this cool profession where you can learn new things and grow exponentially. It's fun. Really.

POV:

Moving on to POV, Point of View, there are three main ways you can write novels.

The first is what I call 'I-Yi-Yi' books. First person narrative. I've only done one romance in this format, Gabby's Place. And this was unusual for me. Actually the book is part in first person and part in omniscient, but I think it worked out well. My teen books are all in first person. I read this great book when I was a teen called 'A Worm in the Ear,' and I just loved it. It was in first person and funnier than hell.

Example of First Person: *I went for a walk down by the pier to think.*

Problems with first person writing is that 'I' can be used WAY too much, thus the descriptor 'I-Yi-Yi.' It's a challenge to write first person books, so please keep this in mind! Also, decide whether you'll write in first person for just one character or for all characters.

Second person writing uses the pronoun 'You.' Actually, my last sentence in the paragraph above is a perfect example of this. I don't recall reading any novels in second person, but I'm sure they're out there. I would think this POV would be mostly self-help books.

Example of Second Person: *If you need to think, walk down by the pier.*

Third person limited writing uses the words 'he, she, it' and describes the feelings and thoughts of one person.

Example of Third Person: *Bill walked down by the pier to think.*

Third person omniscient tells us the feelings and thoughts of every person in the novel. This is the most common type of novel, as this POV is very flexible and easier to write than just from one viewpoint.

So the next time you're reading a novel, try to determine what the POV is. With Gabby's Place, I took a risk and began the novel with her point of view, first person, then flipped over to third person from the hero's viewpoint. Sort of unusual, but this turned out to be (my own) most favorite book!! I think it worked well.

Chapter 9

The Beginning

Your book title is so important!!

An example: You're writing a non-fiction book on being organized. You decide to title it "How to be Organized." ZZZZZ. How about "How to be Organized in Three Easy Steps." Or "How to be Organized When You Don't Have Time." Try for some approach that hasn't been done before. Study what's out there and do something different. Make it interesting!!

Fiction, be creative. "Fast Sam." Or maybe "Graduation Blues" or "Easier Ride" if it's a book about motorcycles. Try for something unusual to catch the reader's attention. Two or three words is good.

Aside from your book cover, unusual title and blurb, your actual book beginning has to really grab the reader.

Most authors put their characters in the middle of the action, right from the beginning.

If you publish on Amazon or on other outlets, quite often a portion of your book will be offered for free. Readers can sample your book. And 99 percent of the time, this freebie is at the very start of your book.

The beginning is your golden opportunity to hook the reader, involve the reader, and intrigue the reader, so he or she really wants to buy your book.

How do you do this? You involve the reader by presenting a problem for the hero or heroine to solve. It seems insurmountable, but then you brainstorm and work it out later in the book.

In *Romance for Luke*, the beginning brings a huge snowstorm. Luke finds a little woman whose buggy has crashed, brings her home, and she turns out to be pregnant, ready to deliver. So the reader is left wondering who this woman is, and how on earth he can help her.

In Romance for Matthew, Bethany is a new mother who goes to work as an assistant for Matthew, who is blind. Her baby is small and she's still breastfeeding him. The problem presented in the first chapter is that this is the first time she's away from him, and she doesn't think she can cope.

So the first chapter problem can be mental or physical, or both. It seems insurmountable, but you'll work it out.

When you've delved into the problem from all angles, and you've hopefully hooked the reader, you can back off, and give a little break. Use this time to describe the hero or other characters more fully, as well as scenery descriptions.

Chapter 10

The Middle

The middle of the book is where the hero/heroine's problems are enhanced and made even worse. Other difficulties might arise, and outside factors come into play.

This is a great place to add new and unusual characters. This creates interest. Make sure they are germane to the story and not superfluous bits of fluff.

It's said every character in your story must move the story along to its conclusion. Otherwise, why even bring them in?

An irritant to me, and this is done by a most famous author, is just *naming* a character. Don't do that. People need some type of impression. Right now, I'm reading a beauty and the beast type romance, where the hero has a long scar on his face. Author refers to him as *leonine* (like a lion) which is very descriptive.

Other short descriptors you can use for your characters: tow-headed, dark-haired, formal, slovenly, matron, geezer, suit, flashy, blonde bombshell, hooker, stooped, and so on.

Examples:

Naming - Mr. Klondike was very helpful as he chatted.

Descriptive - The old man, hunching over as he chatted, was very helpful.

Naming - Nelly Flatbush stood in the hallway, impeding their progress, hoping for news.

Descriptive - Nelly, blonde-bombshell resident hooker, posed in the hallway, impeding their progress, hoping for news.

Anyway, hopefully you get the gist of this. A few chosen words for a bit character, and you don't even need a name. Klondike can be 'the old man' and Nelly can be 'the hooker' for the rest of their times in the story!!

If this is your first novel, try to make as few characters as you can get away with. It becomes harder exponentially every time you add a character. You need to keep track of them, how their relating in the story, and their physical location, which can be difficult.

This is where your notebooks can come in handy. One page for each character would probably do it. So if they're in the beginning of the book, then at the end for some reason, you'll have a small character sketch so you don't forget them!!

At any rate, the middle is where you just bury your hero or heroine with problems. Face the readers with difficulties that seem insurmountable. Then, write your way out of it!

As I've said, in the middle of Lacene Lords, I had no idea who had done the murder of Spence's parents. I had to sit and figure that out...

Chapter 11

The End

Okay, here is where you wrap everything up in a nice tidy fiction bow. I've actually made long lists after my first draft of novels called 'loose ends!' Don't leave any, because readers will thrash you in reviews if you do. Readers are very savvy and observant.

Depending on whether you plan to have an Epilogue, this very last chapter should end all problems with the hero or heroine. Dare I say, happily ever after? And if you do plan an Epilogue, leave a few outstanding difficulties which are then solved in the very end.

If you're the organized type, write out all the problems you've presented in your book, each on a 3X5 card, along with the associated characters. Write on the card how you plan to solve the problem, then make a time line sequence of how you are going to do the last chapter.

Most books end up happily ever after, but this is a decision you'll need to make. Some end sadly, with a death or illness. But I think most people like a happy ending, a resolution.

Chapter 12

Epilogue

I always like an epilogue, and I have them in most of my fiction books. It can move forward in time, like a month or a year later. In *Lacene Lords*, when the killer is caught and the house burns, there are still issues. And a few months later, those issues are solved in the epilogue.

If you plan to use an epilogue, leave a few items hanging in the last chapter. Don't wrap up everything there.

You can also hint at a sequel here, perhaps a long-term, long-range problem, with a question attached.

The epilogue can be in a different format from the rest of your book. If you have a third person book, the epilogue can be in first person, with the main character speaking.

There is no right way to write an epilogue, except it must have a purpose: problem solving or character development and growth.

Chapter 13

Editing and Publishing

Editing:

OMG, I could probably write a whole book on editing and be just as bad at it as I am right now!!

I don't think there's a writer alive who enjoys editing, probably because it uses the left brain, and we're more comfortable in right brain.

This is the main gripe I hear about self-published books. There are mistakes, grammatical or sentence problems, formatting mistakes, misspellings, the list goes on and on. At the publishing houses, there are editors for each book. But, if you're an Indy writer, you are your own editor.

If something doesn't seem right in your book, read it over several times, then look for *duplicate words.* In my writer's class in California, I noticed one author ask another how it was going with his novel. He replied, "Just trying to get those dang duplicates out." And I knew exactly what he was talking about, and was interested to find out that I was not the only one who re-used words.

Take the following example:

The bog was seriously green and swampy this time of year. Toads croaked out a loud melody and crickets could be heard as well. Charles thought the bog could seriously use a few gallons of bleach.

Silly example, but you get where I'm going with this!! And the duplicate words can also appear further down in the next or following paragraphs, and still make you feel like something is wrong with that particular page when you're editing.

Comma placement is a real pain. I can only suggest that you read the sentence aloud, and wherever you pause, that's a good place for a comma.

Run-on sentences are common in fiction as are fragmented sentences, and sometimes that's okay. There is a much greater leeway in fiction, for this sort of thing, than non-fiction.

Most grammar problems and misspellings are caught by Microsoft Word, so always research the red or blue underlined areas. However I noticed the following problem with one manuscript on a writer's website for fiction. The Arabs were running through a *bizarre*, which should have been a *bazaar*. A very serious grammar mistake in a book about marketplaces!! So if you're not sure about a word, I suggest Googling it. Also, have a trusted friend read your work to catch those bizarre mistakes...

And, another word about editing. Don't be so in love with your writing that you cannot delete or edit passages. Be brutal.

Publishing

Amazon:

I've been a fan of Amazon publishing website for a while. Amazon just publishes on Amazon, and distributes to no other outlets.

The Amazon publishing software will point out misspellings in your end manuscript which is very handy. Sign up to publish your book on the Amazon website. Just Google 'Amazon KDP' and follow the instructions on *how to publish an e-book.*

One thing you should do before this step, though, is to have a graphic designer make you a professional-looking cover. I always make my own covers, but not everyone has the patience for this. A professional cover can make all the difference in book sales! You can probably get a cover made for $50.

Another thing to research before you actually sign on to publish is pinpointing about seven search terms used for your book. For instance, with this book, I came up with these: How to write and publish a book, How to write a book, How to write a novel, and Writing a book. These terms are what people will key into the search engine to find your book.

Also, if you decide to go through Create-a-Space on Amazon, which is very inexpensive, you'll be able to get a proof *book*, which is awesome. Many times, you'll be able to catch even more mistakes this way, as your book will look different in the printed layout than on the screen. Plus, it's nice to give your readers the option of a printed book *and* an e-book.

Just a word on signing up for KDP, which means that your book will be exclusively distributed on Amazon for 90 days. You will not just get your own book sales but also a portion of the Amazon KDP pot, which is a formula on pages read. So there is the potential there to make a bit more money. The downside is that you cannot publish anywhere else while you're under contract with KDP. You can also offer your book for free as an introductory incentive to your readers, which I do not recommend. (More later on that.) You can still publish a book on Amazon without joining KDP, so ponder that and decide what you'd like to do.

Smashwords

Smashwords is a great way to go, as it publishes on quite a few recognized websites like Barnes and Noble, Apple Books, Kobo,

Oyster, plus many, many more popular outlets, including libraries.

Their software points out formatting errors, as it 'smashes' your words in to a bunch of different formats! And the staff members at Smashwords are awesome, and so helpful if you're having problems.

Just Google 'Smashwords' and follow their instructions for publishing your novel. Your cover should be at least 1800 X 2400 pixels to be accepted, and they have lists of reputable graphic design artists for your cover, as well as established Smashwords authors who can assist you with formatting problems. I've found Smashwords to be very user friendly, and they have detailed instructions on publishing your book and also a video. Signing up is free and publication is also free.

Both Amazon and Smashwords give you free reporting on your book sales on a daily, weekly and monthly basis. They also both pay on a monthly basis, which is awesome and better than conventional publishing houses.

Chapter 14

Making Money at It

This is when I will try to convince you, unless you're a very prolific author, not to offer your book for free at any time. A few of my books are free, but I also have over 20 books published. For me, it's a way to draw in readership.

This is what will happen if you offer your new book for free, even for a short time:

* Every book shyster on the internet will glom onto your freebie, and will forever offer it on the internet for nothing. And for you to get it off their websites is like Whack-A-Mole. You will, from then on, have no or very few book sales.

* You will get terrible reviews because that's what some people do for kicks. They obtain a free e-book and trash it.

* People will think your book is worthless.

So now you're wondering about pricing. How much should you ask for your book? Keep in mind that if you're an unknown author, and if you over-price your book, you'll have trouble selling copies.

The first consideration is length. Smashwords staff did an extensive study on e-book pricing, and they found the sweet spot is $2.99. However, if your book is a 600 page novel or a long non-fiction book, you'll need to ask more. I've seen $2.99 books with just 20 pages, which seems ridiculous. If I wrote a book that short, I'd ask $.99 for sure.

Another factor you need to study is what books of this type are selling for. For instance, look up Fashion self-help books if that's the type you're writing, and see what they're going for. If similar books are selling (have reviews also) for $9.99 and the length is approximately the same as yours, think about pricing in that range.

Romance books are all over the map, but the great majority go for $2.99. What lots of romance authors do is offer their first romances for free *after they write their second and third book*, to bring in readers.

Non-fiction book prices vary widely, so the best idea is to research.

Creating a website and being active on social media like Facebook, Twitter and Pinterest will sell tons of books. Amazon and Twitter also have specific ads you can create to promote your books, but that will take some money. Social media is free, so begin there.

The bookstores may let you do a book signing, if you go through Create-A-Space and cut them in on the profits for the books you're able to sell.

Another factor in publishing is the first 30-90 days. The very first days your book is published are critical. Everything must be perfect for the great debut: cover, edited manuscript, etc. If your book is going to take off, the first 30 days will probably cause that to happen. People eagle-eye all the new books. Amazon has special categories for 30, 60 and 90 days new books, which many people peruse.

And if you're able to coordinate your book publishing with social media, you'll be that much further ahead.

Study Twitter, follow other authors and see what they're doing there. See their tweets and followers.

Pinterest has loads of book categories you can pin and add your books to.

Facebook is great for letting your friends and family know what's happening and that you're publishing. It never hurts to have friends and family buy a copy of your book and give a short review.

Just a word about reviews. If you study the book reviews on Amazon and other places, there is something odd about a little-known author having all five-star reviews. Even the famous authors have varied reviews, even two and three stars.

And if you do get iffy reviews from regular readers, pay attention. I've actually re-written endings and other parts of my books because I thought reviewers were correct in their assessments!!

However, I'd urge you to NOT respond to any type of negative reviews. This is never done. It's hard not to respond, especially when it's obvious that the reader hasn't read your book. But be the bigger person and ignore nasty reviews.

Another avenue for book promotion is the local newspaper. Write or e-mail the person in charge of the Entertainment section with your name, the name of your new book and all the associated details. If you have a hard copy, a Create-a-Space copy or other, send that along too.

Make yourself some professional-looking business cards, with 'Author,' your name and website or e-mail, and hand them out liberally. Maybe have a promotion, like 50% reduced price or similar. Smashwords has special coupons for your books that you can create and e-mail to people.

You are your own best promoter. Even if you snag a publishing contract, you will probably need to do the majority of your own book promotion.

Chapter 15

Protecting Your Work

Long story short, in 2012, I'd had my second book for free on Ibooks and it was extremely popular, with 35,000 downloads and garnering 600+ good reviews. One day, I happened to notice a book similar to mine in Amazon's search parameters.

Upon researching this, another woman (and I use this term loosely) author had blatantly copied my book, which I saw in that search page. After buying a copy, I saw that the plot was identical and in some areas of her book, even the dialogue was exactly the same!!

Needless to say, I was devastated. I wrote to Amazon first, then wrote to the woman's publisher. And, guess what? There was nothing I could do about it, without going to court and incurring huge legal fees. What made it worse was the woman was a porno author, with all that implies...

I went on Amazon's author website, venting, and told everyone what happened. One author replied this way: "There are only three plots: Man gets girl, man loses girl, and man kills whale." Well, I thought that was the funniest thing I'd seen in a while and it totally put this in perspective for me.

It is very devastating when your book is copied in such a blatant way. But in hindsight, first, I shouldn't have offered the book for free. That was a mistake. Second, I decided that I would continue publishing books, which I did. And, hopefully, my new books would not be copied by her. But I never checked on that. It wasn't worth my time. And I knew, with my imagination, that I was a much better author than she was. She knows what she is, and I know what I am.

As well, one more very interesting thing happened in 2014. I sometimes Google my name to make sure my books are accessible. And one day, I saw that a book *I hadn't even published yet* was being offered on a French website. I had loaded it, *partially completed*, onto Amazon and Smashwords, as this sometimes helps me with editing. But how these dopes were able to access my unpublished book is a mystery to me and to both publishing websites. Very peculiar. I still haven't published that book.

What I'm getting at here is that you cannot protect your work!! Once you publish, and it's out there on the internet, people are free to copy any part of it. They aren't supposed to, but what starving author can afford to hire an attorney every time a copycat surfaces?? And these imitator idiots are probably aware of that.

I truly hope this never happens to you!! And, if it should, try to be the bigger person.

Chapter 16

The End...or is it The Beginning?

So now, I can hear you protesting that you have no spare time to write a book. Let me ask some questions. Do you sleep until the very last moment in the morning? How many hours do you watch TV every day? How many weekends do you spend just shopping?

There are twenty-four hours in a day. Eight of those hours are often spent working for someone else. Eight hours are spent sleeping. That leaves you eight more hours, and somewhere within those extra eight hours, you can write. An hour or two a day is totally doable!! You just have to make it happen.

Now, back to the ending. There is a real letdown sometimes after you finish a book. You feel at loose ends, and very sad. This is common and understandable. Your focus for months has ended. You wonder what will happen next. You've been going at full speed, 100 miles an hour for a while, and now the brakes are on. Everything seems blah.

Try to focus on this end time as a true beginning. Let your imagination loose. Do you want to do a sequel? I've done three Whirlwind Passing books, umpteen romance books, a kid's Dream Club series, and self-help books. And it seemed to flow naturally at the time. Sometimes one would lead to another. You have ultimate possibilities, they are endless, with all the plots and heroes and villains.

When in doubt, write!! It will do you good and you'll make your *footprint* in the world. And when you pass away, a bit of you will be left behind in the form of your books. You will have accomplished amazing things. I truly hope you are a wonderful success at book writing.

But remember. Persistence. Don't give up. Ever!

THE END

Join me on Twitter at fornat2003 and Pinterest

Other books by Nancy Fornataro:

<u>Closet Evolution</u>

A natural progression of the 'old' way of arranging your closet into the new *revolutionary closet style*!

You will spend less on clothes
You will know exactly what clothes you need to buy
You will be able to travel on a moment's notice

You'll look pulled together every day
Maintaining your closet will be a snap
Dressing will be a breeze
Everything in your closet will be wearable
You'll have a 50% increase in closet space
You will easily design your wardrobe
You will control your closet instead of it controlling you

How to Look Like a Million on Next to Nothing

Short on cash but want to look your best? Confused whenever you go into your closet?

How to Look Like a Million will answer *these questions:*

* What clothes should I buy and when?

* Where should I buy my clothes?

* How much makeup should I wear?

* Why can't I get my closet under control?

* What's wrong with buying basic beige?

* Which clothes should I keep and which should I throw out?

* What is Collection Dressing exactly?

* How can I learn to comparison shop?

* What are wardrobe basics?

* How much jewelry should I wear?

* How can I successfully pack for a trip?

* Which storage containers should I use for my clothes?

* What can I do with off-season clothes?

* What does dressing have to do with bulletin boards?

* Why shouldn't I shop for clothes at thrift stores?

These questions will be answered, and many more. After you read this book, you'll have confidence and style, day after day, year after year, using Collection Dressing.

Enhance your wardrobe.
Have a fully functional closet.
Be ready for any situation.

Start right now!!!

Organize your Clothes Closet

Are you *Wardrobe Challenged*?

If so, this book will answer the following questions:

** What are wardrobe basics?

** What accessories should I use?

** Should I keep this item, or toss it?

** What areas of my wardrobe can I spend less on?

** How much should I spend on my clothes?

** Where are my wardrobe holes?

** What are my colors?

** What season am I?

** What should I buy the next time I go clothes shopping?

** How should I rearrange my closet for maximum results?

By the end of this book, you'll understand your wardrobe and what to shop for on your next trip.

By using G-O-T C-L-A-S-S system for the one-day cleaning blitz and N-O W-A-Y G-I-R-L, the ultimate way to weed and cull your wardrobe, you'll be ready for any situation that comes your way.

Organize Yourself A - Z
One Day at a Time!!

The perfect gift for yourself... an organized life.

Think you're organized? Not necessarily!!

Have you looked at your file folders lately? Know what's in any of them? And your dresser drawers...are they sectioned, with the contents neatly folded by type and color or just a mishmash of various items?

Do you walk out of the house every day, wearing wrinkled clothes? Do you have a wardrobe inventory, and know exactly what to buy when you clothes shop? Still using wire hangers? Where are your wardrobe 'holes?'

This book will help you:

* Shop wisely and save hundreds of dollars every year.

* Organize your home, one section at a time.

* Schedule your precious time.

* Keep track of important paperwork.

* Clean, without using harsh products.

New and unusual tips for :

* Cleaning old, fiberglass bathtubs
* Using baggies wisely
* Decorating with baskets
* Eliminating hard water stains
* Making your bedroom an oasis
* Unusual room dividers

Simplify your life for maximum enjoyment:

"I realized a while back that I had too much stuff. Me? The original organized person? How could this be??

Then I thought back to my various moves, and realized that for years I'd been toting this stuff along with me from place to place!

And, if that wasn't bad enough, I had too many "organizer contraptions" for my own good. Which led me to my next realization: You cannot get organized unless you purge your stuff.

So, I was basically a closet hoarder. If you visited my house during those years, you would have thought I was very organized...but what went on inside closets, file cabinets and drawers, you don't want to know!!

The silly part of it was I always saw myself as an organizer. Everything was always neat on the surface of my life, but as I delved deeper to the interior, it was downright scary.

And it all started with my bedroom closet, along with yet another move. My book "Organize Your Clothes Closet" was just the beginning. From there I branched out to the garage, then the kitchen and bathrooms.

Within these pages you will find an assortment of good tips on organizing. Believe me when I say, I have worked these steps, and my house and my life are 100% better. And, best of all, these things work because I've tried them all."

Thrifty Decorating

Given up on keeping your house in order and decorated nicely? Think you can't afford to fix it up? Don't have the time? Think again!! This handy book will show you the way.

"Part of my thrifty nature comes from the thrill of the hunt. There's nothing that pleases me more than to find an item I need for the house for one-half or one-third the retail price. Face it, wouldn't you rather have a diamond ring or a snazzy coat because you didn't pay full price for items in your house and you have extra money now? And still have your house looking great? Yep, that's

us…just you and me. You have the will and I'll show you the way."

Romance:

Nicky's Fire (A Contemporary Romance):
Two DEA agents: Nick (Bad Boy) and Chloe (Good Girl) thrown together on assignment. Bikers. Fights. Outdoor concerts by The Rocker (semi-Bad Boy) along with DEA Supervisor (Good Girl) sparks fly!!

Romance in Hollywood - The Director:
Ever wonder what goes on behind the scenes in a movie? You're about to find out. From stinky leading men, to sex starved extras, exposes, humor on set, and the forever striving towards awards, this is it. Janis 'Baby' Storm, trying to make a comeback, wonders if it's even possible, as she turns to director Holt for guidance.

Romance in Dallas - Tycoon!

Ramsey Knowles amassed great fortune and fame, but at what price? Rich, powerful, successful, he craves the one thing he can't have.

His physical condition creates a need within him to be whole again. But would Jace, a professional in her own right, be the one to fulfill it? Jacine seeks to help him forget his past, and in the process, realizes her own weakness. How could she help him when she couldn't even help herself?

Also:
Gabby's Place - Romance/Suspense
Lacene Lords – (Supernatural – FREE)
Romance in Vegas – Showgirl (FREE)
Romance for Lee - A Christmas Story
Romance for Matthew (Christian romance)
Romance for Luke (Historical romance - FREE)
Romance for Kinkade (Historical romance)

Whirlwind Passing - Death Kiss (Detective – FREE)

Whirlwind Passing - Pyro! (Detective)

From Above - Sunset of the World (Whirlwind Passing)